How Does Wi-Fi Work?

by Mark Weakland

CAPSTONE PRESS
a capstone imprint

Capstone Captivate is published by Capstone Press, an imprint of Capstone.
1710 Roe Crest Drive
North Mankato, Minnesota 56003
www.capstonepub.com

Library of Congress Cataloging-in-Publication Data is available on the Library of Congress website.
ISBN: 978-1-4966-8071-6 (library binding)
ISBN: 978-1-4966-8713-5 (paperback)
ISBN: 978-1-4966-8167-6 (eBook PDF)

Summary: You probably use Wi-Fi all the time to connect to the internet through your laptop, tablet, or phone. It's easy. Wi-Fi hotspots surround you as you go through your day—from school to a pizza place or coffee shop and then back home. Not so long ago, the internet wasn't as accessible. Find out how Wi-Fi works, how it became commonplace, and what it might do for you in the future.

Image Credits
Alamy: Andrew Cheal, 23, TP, 4 (bottom right); Getty Images: Bob Rowan, 8, Hulton Deutsch, 14, Peathegee Inc, 42, Stringer/David Becker, 28; iStockphoto: Alfribeiro, 33, artbyjulie, 17 (map), Media Raw Stock, 39, pop_jop, 12; Newscom: WENN/Toasteroid/ZCHE, 29, ZUMA Press/ JT Vintage, 13; Pixabay: Clker-Free-Vector-Images, cover (house icon), Fauno, 9 (all), 36 (all), paulnaude, cover; Shutterstock: Alex Murphy, 37 (bottom), Andrey Popov, 5, attraction art, 27, badahos, 11, Beatriz Vera, 31, Dr Project, 35, Gabor Tinz, 26, Kaspars Grinvalds, 25, Krunja, 18, LIORIKI, background (circuit board), mentatdgt, 24, metamorworks, 41, mStudioVector, 4 (top), muratart, 10, Ohmega1982, 44–45, ra2 studio, 21, 34, Reservoir Dots, 17 (antennas), sirtravelalot, 7, small smiles, 30, Svitlana Amelina, 4 (bottom left), taa22, 40, Vasily Makarov, 37 (top), View Apart, 20, ZadarmA Creation, 19

Editorial Credits
Editor: Leah Kaminski; Designer: Sara Radka; Media Researcher: Eric Gohl; Production Specialist: Kathy McColley

Table of Contents

Words in **bold** are in the glossary.

What Is Wi-Fi?

What do a phone, a toaster, and a dog collar have in common? These very different objects can share one high-tech feature. They can connect to the internet through **Wi-Fi**.

This is the Wi-Fi symbol. You see it everywhere. It is pasted on the doors of coffee shops. It glows on the screens of computers and tablets.

HIGH-TECH FACT

The original Wi-Fi logo was based on the yin-yang symbol.

Wi-Fi is a simple word with a complex meaning. To learn all about it, let's look inside a laptop and see how Wi-Fi works. Let's discover the places Wi-Fi exists. And let's see the amazing things Wi-Fi can do. Here's a little preview:

Many home appliances, including refrigerators, now use Wi-Fi.

- With Wi-Fi, you can learn the top speed of a jet-powered go-cart. (It's a little more than 112 miles (180 kilometers) per hour.)

- With Wi-Fi, your refrigerator can order frozen pizza from the supermarket. Yum!

- With Wi-Fi, you can find your lost dog. Here, Sparky! Here, boy!

CHAPTER 1

No Wires for Wi-Fi

Wi-Fi is sometimes called "wireless internet." Through the internet, information is shared. The information can be words or pictures. It can be music or video. With Wi-Fi, a mobile phone or computer can connect to the internet and join in the sharing. The connection is strong and steady. Best of all, no wires are needed.

Wires, Wires Everywhere

Before Wi-Fi came along, devices were connected through wires. Computers had them sprouting from their back panels. These wires connected to other wires in the wall. They were then strung to wires on poles outside. These far-flung wires linked computers in distant places.

In time, thousands of computers were connected. They formed a kind of giant web. This became the internet. Through this web of computers, information was created and shared.

HIGH-TECH FACT

When you ask a question on Google, your computer electronically searches about 1,000 computers. On average, it takes 0.2 seconds to get an answer.

Ethernet cables were the most common cable internet link before Wi-Fi was widespread.

Connecting all these computers took a lot of wires. And all the wires led to lots of troubles. Wires twisted and tangled. They got in the way when you moved around. Sometimes they broke. Wi-Fi was a solution to these problems.

Students had to use computer labs to access the internet in the 1990s.

Devices Unleashed

Before Wi-Fi, devices stayed in one place. For example, a computer sat on a desk. It connected to the internet only through a cable. Because of the cable, the computer could not be moved. This meant you could not send messages while standing in the kitchen. You could not play internet games while sitting in a car. And you could not research a school paper while lying in your bed. Everything had to be done at the computer on the desk.

Wi-Fi Does Not Stand for Other Words

Many debate about what the word Wi-Fi stands for. Some say it stands for wireless fidelity. That wording is a lot like the real term high fidelity or hi-fi. That is an older term that refers to high sound quality. But others say Wi-Fi doesn't stand for anything! They say it was just a silly-sounding word that a company made up. Because it was fun to say, people remembered it.

A cable-connected computer is like a dog on a leash. It can only move so far. But get rid of the leash and the dog can run everywhere. Using Wi-Fi is like letting a dog off its leash. Today, devices go everywhere. People put their phones in their pockets. They carry their laptops in their backpacks. Through Wi-Fi, mobile devices connect to the internet. When your phone or computer is within range of a Wi-Fi **network**, just press a button to connect!

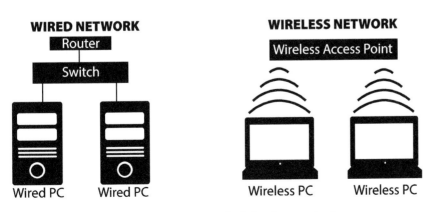

Wired networks can be more reliable than wireless ones.

CHAPTER 2

The Roots of Wi-Fi

With Wi-Fi, messages and information are carried by invisible waves. The waves are sent through an antenna. Then they zip through the air to another antenna. Sending waves through the air is called **broadcasting**. No wires are needed with Wi-Fi. But this is not how things were always done.

Some radio antennas are on towers that are more than 2,000 feet (610 meters) tall.

Sending Information Long Ago

Thousands of years ago, people transmitted information only through word of mouth. Say someone saw a tiger attacking people in the forest. To get this information to the king, the person would run until he got to the village. There, the person would say, "A tiger is attacking people in the forest!"

Much later, people sent information by letters. Letters were handwritten and then carried by people from one place to another. Letters could also be carried on ships across the ocean. Sometimes, it took weeks or months to deliver a letter. Later still, after the discovery of electricity, people learned how to send information over wires. This was a much faster way to communicate.

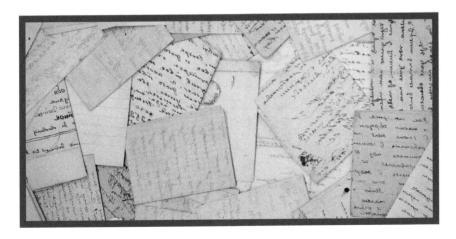

Before the invention of the automobile, letters were often delivered by horse and carriage.

Radio Waves

The seeds of Wi-Fi were planted in the late 1800s. At the time, wires large and small carried information. Thin strands of copper wire sent messages called telegraphs across the United States. One monstrous cable made of copper and steel lay on the floor of the Atlantic Ocean. It carried telegraph messages between Europe and North America.

Electromagnetic Radiation

Radio waves are a kind of **electromagnetic radiation**. This type of radiation spans everything from X-rays to radio waves. It also includes visible light. Electromagnetic radiation exists as waves of energy. Every type of wave has a height and a length. Radio waves are the longest.

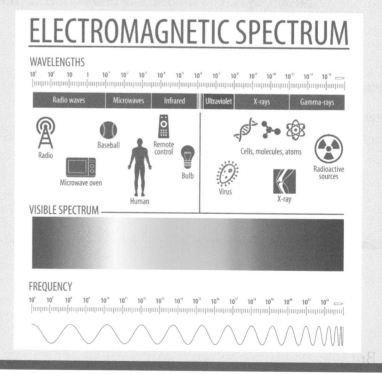

Around the same time, a man named Heinrich Hertz was experimenting with electromagnetic waves. Hertz wanted to prove these waves were similar to heat and light waves. He used homemade gadgets to experiment. When he put his gadgets to work, sparks flew. Electricity buzzed. Most importantly, electromagnetic waves were produced. Later, these waves were called radio waves.

Radio waves were first called Hertzian waves, after Heinrich Hertz.

Hertz never thought about how his invisible waves could be used in practical ways. Another man had to figure out how radio waves could carry information and replace wires.

Signals from Afar

Guglielmo Marconi was an Italian inventor. He showed that radio waves could send and receive telegraph messages. His first radio signals traveled less than a mile. But later, his radio system transmitted a signal across the Atlantic Ocean. The message it carried was simply the letter *s*. The wave traveled from England to Canada. That is more than 2,000 miles (3,219 km)!

HIGH-TECH FACT

To send a radio wave across the ocean, Marconi used a 500-foot antenna strung from a giant kite.

Marconi received radio waves on a Canadian island called Newfoundland, which is one of the closest locations to England in North America.

In time, radio waves carried more and more messages and information. First they transmitted words and sentences using the dots and dashes of telegraph language. Then, they carried **audio** information. This meant that voices and music could be heard on a radio. Next came television. Now, people could see moving images. All of this was leading to the day when radio waves would transmit **digital** information stored on computers.

Wireless Telegraphs Timeline

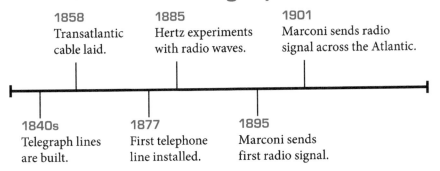

1858
Transatlantic cable laid.

1885
Hertz experiments with radio waves.

1901
Marconi sends radio signal across the Atlantic.

1840s
Telegraph lines are built.

1877
First telephone line installed.

1895
Marconi sends first radio signal.

Radio Waves From Space

Outer space is full of objects that produce radio waves. Stars and galaxies make them. So do black holes. Like Wi-Fi signals, these radio waves carry information. The information tells scientists what the object is made of and how hot or cold it is. Scientists gather this information with radio telescopes. By studying radio waves from space, scientists learn how stars work and what planets are made of.

Wi-Fi Across the Decades

The first wireless network was built in 1971. Its name was ALOHAnet. The scientists who created it worked at the University of Hawaii. The university was spread across many islands. How could its computers be connected? Scientists thought of using radio waves.

They also thought of sending information in packets rather than bit by bit. This way, more information could be moved. Scientists also created ways for a computer to automatically transmit information. One person called this invention earth-shattering! Why? One reason is that it led to the wireless internet.

Over the next 30 years, researchers and **engineers** worked on the technology. By the late 1990s, a system called IEEE 802.11 made sure that all radio wave devices sent and received information in the same way. Engineers could design faster and bigger networks.

Puuwai
Kekaha
NIIHAU
KAL

HIGH-TECH FACT
One radio wave can be 60 miles (97 km) long, or longer!

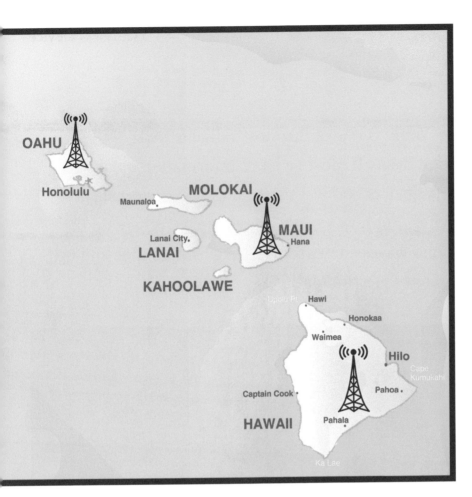

ALOHAnet allowed users on other islands to connect to the computers at the University of Hawaii's main campus on Oahu.

IEEE 802.11 was a big step forward. But the name was a mouthful to say. In 1999, someone came up with the name Wi-Fi. The name stuck.

HIGH-TECH FACT

Radio telescopes detect radio waves from galaxies far, far away. The waves take millions of years to reach Earth.

CHAPTER 3
How Wi-Fi Works

Wi-Fi is one of the most valuable tools of the digital age. It moves a lot of information quickly. It lets devices connect through radio waves instead of wires. But how exactly does it work? Where do the radio waves come from? And where do they end up going? Let's find out!

Wi-Fi networks can cover areas as small as one apartment or as large as a whole city.

Wi-Fi networks can include security systems, speakers, and game consoles.

Wi-Fi Networks

A network is a collection of devices that connect to share information. Every Wi-Fi network consists of two types of devices. One type has Wi-Fi on it. Common examples are computers and printers. These machines produce radio waves. But they don't use the waves to connect to each other directly. They link to each other through a second type of device. It's called a **router**. A Wi-Fi router sends and receives digital information or data in the form of radio waves. More than one device can connect to a router in a network.

HIGH-TECH FACT

There are more than 9 billion Wi-Fi devices in the world today.

The first "internet phone" was released in 1996, but it was very expensive.

It's true that this data can travel through wires. Wires are how a router connects to the internet, in fact. And wires still connect some routers to computers and printers. But most connect through radio waves. This is what happens when a router links to a printer or computer with Wi-Fi. Wi-Fi connections are easier for users, who can move their devices about freely.

Radio Waves Are the Heart of Wi-Fi

To more fully understand how Wi-Fi works, let's look at how a laptop computer sends data. A laptop first stores digital information or data in its memory system. The data exists as a long string of numbers. People never see these numbers. That is because computers translate them into pictures, videos, printed words, and recorded sounds. But in its original form, data is a long string of simple numbers.

Computer data and computer code might be thought of as instructions for tasks a computer can do.

HIGH-TECH FACT
Your body can act as a radio antenna. Bring your hand close to a radio, and you will improve reception.

The simple numbers of computer data are easy to transmit or move from one place to another. Years ago, these numbers only traveled through wires and cables. Now, Wi-Fi enables laptops to move data through the air. But first, a laptop must turn its data into radio waves. This is done through a wireless adapter. Some adapters look like a tiny library card covered in silver wires.

Data in the form of radio waves is beamed out through a small antenna. The waves zoom through the air. An antenna on a router picks up the waves. The router then turns the radio waves back into long strings of numbers. Finally, this is sent to the internet using a cable or wire.

Devices with Wi-Fi can send and receive data. To do this, the process is reversed.

Wireless adapters and wireless network cards contain tiny antennas.

CHAPTER 4
The Many Uses of Wi-Fi

The most popular use of Wi-Fi is to connect machines to the internet. This can happen almost anywhere. You can connect a laptop while sitting in a coffee shop. You can connect a smartphone while strolling through a supermarket, and a tablet while lounging next to a hotel pool.

There is no doubt that connecting to the internet is handy and helpful. But there are other ways Wi-Fi makes life easy for us.

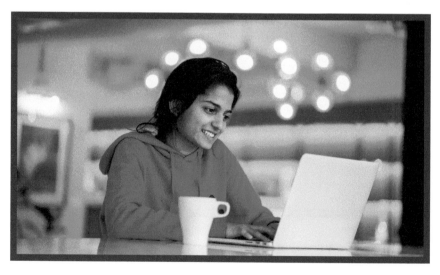

Before Wi-Fi, the only way to get online at a coffee shop was to go to a special "internet café" where internet-connected computers were available.

Common Uses for Wi-Fi

Send Documents to a Printer. Let's say you wrote a story on a computer. Now you want to print it. Wi-Fi lets you print without connecting the two machines with a cable. Your story is sent from the computer to the printer with radio waves.

Stream Movies. You probably **stream** video at home. The video comes from the internet. It is then broadcast over Wi-Fi to another device. The video can be watched on a TV, computer, or tablet. No clunky cables are needed.

Streaming video on your personal device would not be possible without Wi-Fi.

Stream Audio. Wi-Fi lets people stream audio to speakers. Wireless speakers pick up Wi-Fi signals and turn them into sounds. Things were different 30 years ago. Back then, wires connected music players to speakers.

Uncommon Uses of Wi-Fi

Electronic door locks can be outfitted with Wi-Fi. Why would this be helpful? Let's say you go to the movies. Once there, you can't remember if you locked the door. A Wi-Fi connection lets you use your phone to check if your door is locked. It is! If your brother comes home and can't remember the door code, you can unlock it for him.

You can set some smart locks to lock your door as soon as your cell phone leaves the area.

Smart sprinklers help people conserve water. Other Wi-Fi-enabled devices aid in conservation too. For example, smart thermostats can help you save energy when heating and cooling your home.

Another unusual use of Wi-Fi is in a lawn sprinkler. Imagine you are visiting a friend in another state. You check the weather and learn that it is raining back home. Using your phone, you can turn off your sprinkler. Or the sprinkler can use a computer program to sense weather conditions. It then automatically adjusts the amount of water being used. If it is dry, the sprinkler sends out more water. If it is wet, it sends less.

Strange and Silly Wi-Fi

Like anything in life, Wi-Fi can be overused. Some people say it solves problems that are not really problems. Used in some machines, it can waste your money, make you lazy, or both. Here are two examples. Read them and see what you think.

Wi-Fi Toaster. How do you find out if your toast is done? Most people stand next to their toaster and wait for the toast to pop up. But if you don't want to do this, a Wi-Fi toaster will send a signal to your phone. Ding! Now you know your toast is done. Or your toaster can send you a message. "Dear Shayna. Your toast is done."

Wi-Fi toasters can remember what kind of bread you use.

You can tell a Wi-Fi toaster what kind of bread you're toasting with an app, so it perfectly cooks it.

Some Wi-Fi toasters do more. One receives messages sent by friends. The messages are sent through a phone or computer. The Wi-Fi toaster then prints the messages on your toast. Bing! Your toast is done. You pick it up and read, "Good morning, BFF. What's up?"

Wi-Fi Fork. Do you loudly slurp while eating noodles? Or do you quietly eat, cringing while others noisily smack their lips? Inventors in Japan have come up with a way to help both kinds of people.

The solution to the problem of loud noodle slurping is the Otohiko fork. It looks something like a battery-powered toothbrush. What does it do? First it detects slurping noises. Then it connects to your smartphone through Wi-Fi. If your slurp is too loud, it commands your phone to emit a stream of noise. The noise cancels out loud slurping sounds.

Right now, you have to imagine all of this. The fork is only sold in Japan.

The Otohiko fork detects slurping through a microphone in its handle.

Furbo

A gadget called Furbo helps you visit with your dog when you are far away. Furbo connects to the internet through Wi-Fi. This means you can move the device to any place in your home or yard. If your dog barks, Furbo lets you know. Next, press a button on your phone to see video of your pooch. Then, press the microphone button and talk to your pet. And if your dog is being good? Press a third button and Furbo tosses your dog a treat!

Furbo is not the only interactive pet camera. Some even allow you to use a laser pointer to play with your dog over the internet.

CHAPTER 5
Wi-Fi Problems, Wi-Fi Solutions

Radio waves should flow quickly and smoothly between Wi-Fi devices. But they don't always do this. Building a well-running Wi-Fi network is a challenge. Problems pop up. People who design Wi-Fi networks find out where the difficulties are. Then, they do their best to fix them.

So Many Devices

Wi-Fi networks often contain many devices. Every Wi-Fi-enabled device sends out a stream of radio waves. These devices can be printers, computers, smartphones, and more. The router of a network receives the waves. When only a few Wi-Fi devices are in use, the waves easily flow through the network. This is known as a "fast" connection.

But what happens when many devices are using one network? Many devices mean many waves. Too many waves can slow down the router as it works to receive and transmit data. Imagine lots of cars and trucks using a one-lane road. The road is clogged. Traffic creeps along.

Most home networks can support dozens of devices, but this much traffic may result in a slow connection.

Devices that are near the Wi-Fi router often get the fastest speeds by using a 5 gigahertz wavelength.

Things get even worse when the waves are all the same **wavelength**. When waves are the same length, they interfere with each other. Picture a lot of big trucks all trying to use that one-lane road. They cut each other off. Only some can get through.

One way to solve the problem is to use waves of different wavelengths. It's like taking some of those big trucks off the road and replacing them with small cars. This reduces crowding. It cuts down on interference. And it helps information flow back and forth more quickly.

A Cluttered Landscape

In the open air, a typical Wi-Fi router can send a signal at least 300 feet (91 meters). The radio waves are strong and easy to find. Then why can it be difficult to find a Wi-Fi signal in an office building? Walls reflect radio waves. Materials in ceilings and floors block waves. When there are many obstacles, the range of a Wi-Fi network can be much smaller than 300 feet (91 meters). People who design Wi-Fi networks solve this problem by adding more routers.

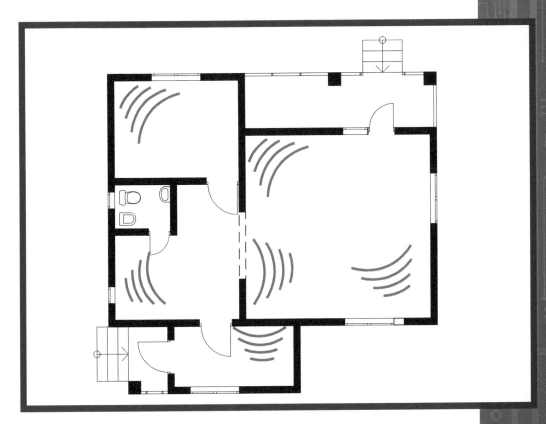

Newer buildings are designed with Wi-Fi in mind, but most older buildings have many obstacles to a clear Wi-Fi signal.

Data Thieves

Have you ever eaten at a McDonald's? If you have, you may have connected to Wi-Fi while you were there. Most McDonald's provide free Wi-Fi. Their network is known as a public network. Anyone with a Wi-Fi device can connect to it.

If you use a public network, be careful. The information flowing through it is usually not **encrypted**. This means it is not protected by security codes. Clever **cybercriminals** might be able to look at your information. They might even steal it. Criminals can hack into public routers. From there, they can gain access to your Wi-Fi-connected phone or laptop. You should never send private information through a public network. Carefully choose what networks you connect to.

Bluetooth Network

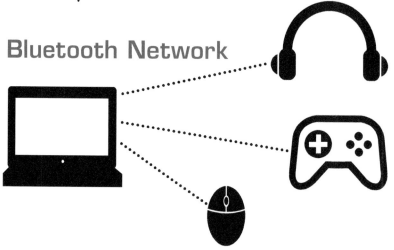

36

Bluetooth headphones are one of the most common uses of the technology.

Many home and business Wi-Fi networks can only be accessed with a password. This is true for schools too. Passwords help keep networks private. Only people with the password can get on the network.

Bluetooth

Bluetooth is another way for devices to connect without wires. Like Wi-Fi, it uses radio waves to do the connecting. Unlike Wi-Fi, it is not used to connect to the internet. Instead, it connects devices to each other. For example, Bluetooth works well for connecting a smartphone to headphones. Bluetooth works best at short distances and when security is not an issue.

CHAPTER 6
Wi-Fi in the Future

Wi-Fi networks have changed a lot since ALOHAnet was first created. Today, Wi-Fi exists on everything from phones to forks. These devices make use of many radio wavelengths. The routers used in Wi-Fi networks are also more advanced. They can "talk" to Wi-Fi devices through better **software** and **hardware**.

IEEE 802.11 continues to be updated to this day. A new version called Wi-Fi 6 can talk to multiple devices at once, instead of one at a time. More wavelengths will become available for devices to use. All of these changes make connections stronger and faster. What will things look like in 20 years?

Smart homes would not be possible without fast, reliable, and secure home Wi-Fi networks.

Everything Has Wi-Fi

Today, it is possible for your home to be full of machines connected to the internet through Wi-Fi. In the future, there will be more and more of these devices. Devices inside your refrigerator and cupboard will scan what is inside. If you are out of cheese, they will send your phone an alert via Wi-Fi. If your cupboard finds no pasta and sauce, it will order some. A smart water system will detect leaks and shut off valves. You will check on your pets when you are away. And your parents will monitor you if you are home by yourself.

Someday, AI will do more than basic tasks.
It may even be creative and emotional.

There are already many kitchen appliances large and small that connect to Wi-Fi.

Artificial Intelligence

Artificial intelligence (AI) describes computer programs that do things only humans can do. Some of these things are speaking, seeing, and making decisions. Today, AI is paired with Wi-Fi. This lets devices respond to human needs, such as getting a weather report or turning on the house lights.

In the future, Wi-Fi and AI will work together to create a fast and smart network. A faster network that works better will allow you to use even more smart home devices. This combination could do a lot of thinking for you. It might look and sound like this:

Your alarm goes off at 6:30 a.m. Your bedroom lights slowly brighten.

"Why are you getting me up so early?" you mumble.

Someday, even your countertop might be computerized and connected to Wi-Fi.

"I scanned your school calendar," says a voice in the ceiling. "Today is school picture day." A door by your closet pops open. "I've picked out your favorite clothes. I've noticed you wear your purple pants a lot."

Before you dress, you shuffle off to the bathroom. You hear water hissing in the shower. "It's not too hot," says the voice. "Just as you like it."

"Thank you," you reply.

Later, you enter the kitchen and head to the refrigerator. "You should drink some orange juice," says the voice. "I am sensing your temperature is higher than it should be. You may be coming down with a cold."

You sit and slurp your cereal and drink your juice. "Your mom will be down in a moment," says the voice. "I've put her clothes out. And I've sent digital money to the school to pay for your pictures. Don't forget to smile!"

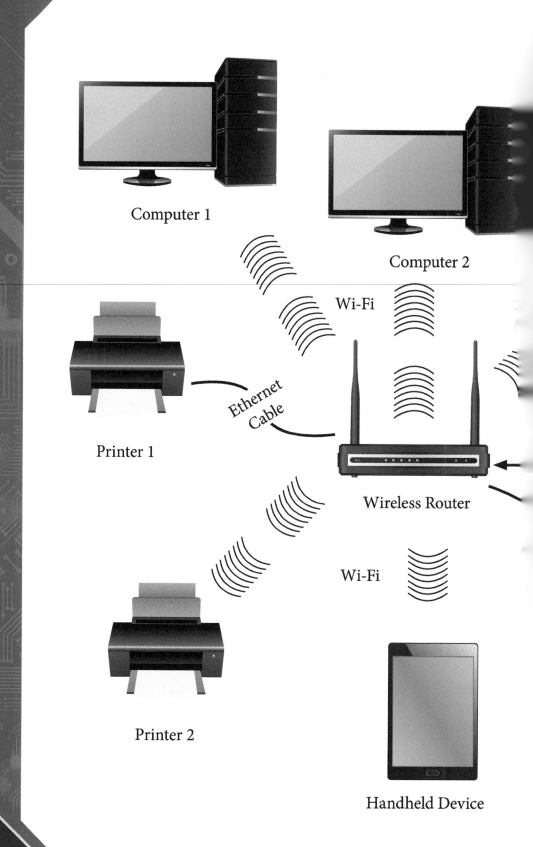

Computer 1

Computer 2

Wi-Fi

Ethernet Cable

Printer 1

Wireless Router

Wi-Fi

Printer 2

Handheld Device

Wi-Fi Network

Laptop Computer

Internet

Wi-Fi

Modem

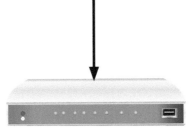

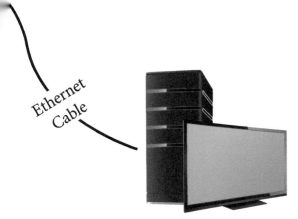

Ethernet Cable

Computer 3

GLOSSARY

artificial intelligence (ar-ti-FISH-uhl in-TEL-uh-junss)—computer systems able to perform tasks that normally require human intelligence

audio (AW-dee-oh)—sound humans can hear

broadcast (BRAHD-kast)—to send signals or programs from a radio or television transmitter

cybercriminal (SY-buhr-kri-muh-nuhl)—a person who engages in a crime by means of computers or the internet

digital (DI-juh-tuhl)—information dealing with numbers or digits

electromagnetic radiation (i-lek-troh-mag-NET-ik ray-dee-AY-shuhn)—waves of energy that can be visible or invisible

encrypt (en-KRIPT)—to protect by using security codes

engineer (en-juh-NEER)—someone who uses science and technology to design things

hardware (HARD-wair)—the physical parts of a computer

network (NET-wurk)—a group of things connected in some way

router (ROWT-ur)—a device that collects signals from other devices and then sends the signals to the internet (or vice versa)

software (SAWFT-wair)—computer programs made of lines of instructions for the computer

stream (STREEM)—a steady flow of information; a steady flow of data

Wi-Fi (WAI-fai)— technology that allows computers to communicate with each other wirelessly

READ MORE

Liukas, Linda. *Hello Ruby: Expedition to the Internet.* New York: Feiwel and Friends, 2018.

Liukas, Linda. *Hello Ruby: Journey Inside the Computer.* New York: Feiwel and Friends, 2017.

Macaulay, David. *The Way Things Work Now.* Boston, MA: HMH Books, 2016.

Sirota, Lyn. *Information Waves.* Let's Explore Science. Vero Beach, FL: Rourke Educational Media, 2016.

Wallmark, Laurie. *Grace Hopper: Queen of Computer Code.* New York: Sterling Children's Books, 2017.

INTERNET SITES

The Carnegie Cyber Academy
http://www.carnegiecyberacademy.com/index.html

Wonderville
https://wonderville.org/studentAudience

Engineer Girl
http://www.engineergirl.org

Science Kids, Technology for Kids
http://www.sciencekids.co.nz/technology.html

Ruff Ruffman, Humble Media Genius
https://pbskids.org/fetch/ruff/

INDEX